George Frideric
HANDEL

O BE JOYFUL
IN THE LORD

Chandos Anthem I

HWV 246

Edited by

Friedrich Chrysander

Revised by

Clark McAlister

Vocal Score

Klavierauszug

SERENISSIMA MUSIC, INC.

CONTENTS

Duration: ca.20 minutes

Composed 1717

First performance: 1717-18

London, Harrow

St. Lawrence, Whitchurch

Soli, Chorus, Orchestra, Composer (conductor)

ISBN: 978-1-60874-202-8

O be joyful in the Lord

HWV 246

G. F. Handel

Edited by Friedrich Chrysander
Revised by Clark McAlister
Keyboard part revised by Alex Samarin

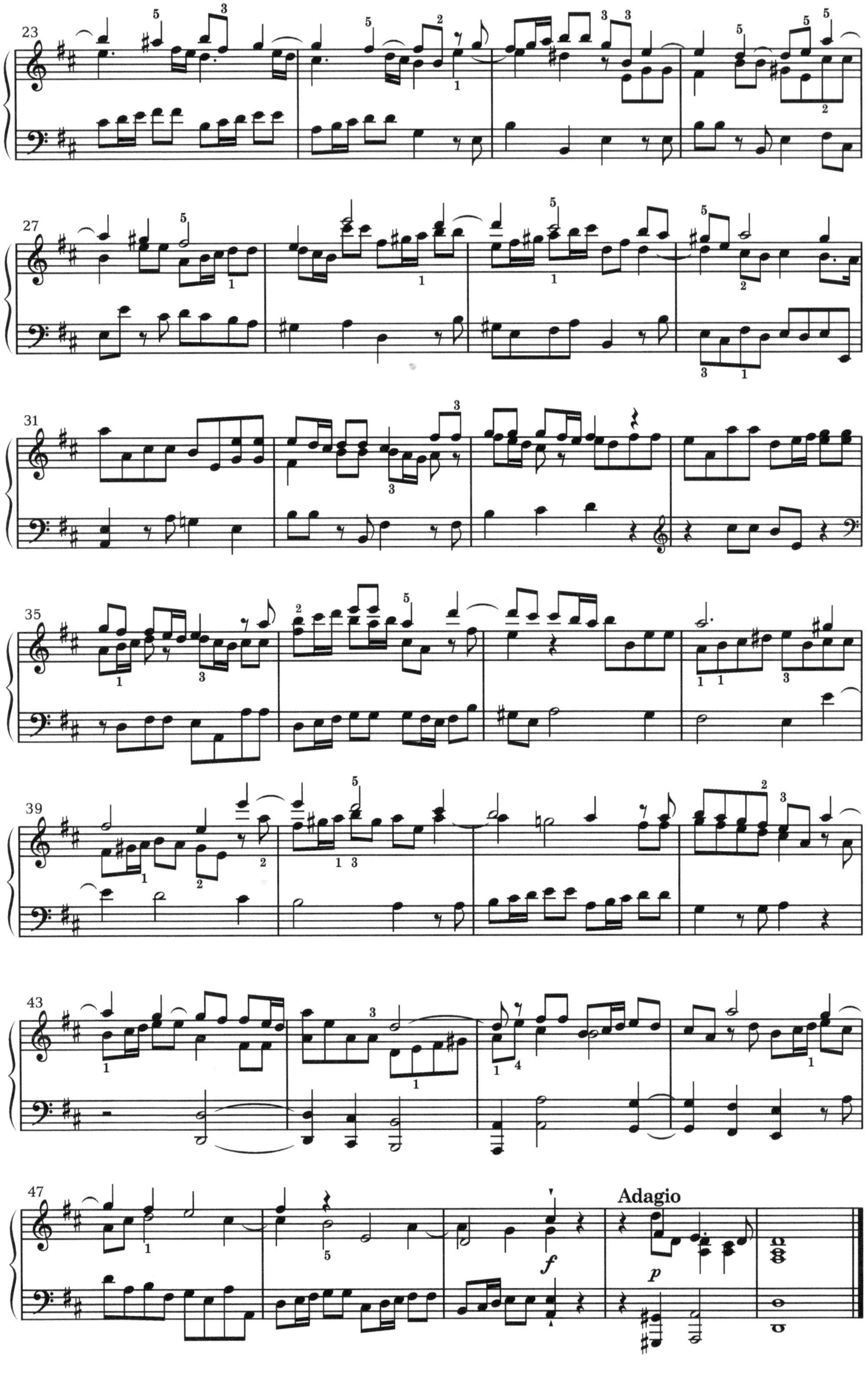
Adagio

2. O, Be Joyful

Tenor Solo

O _____ be

joy - - - - - ful,

Lyrics:
O _____ be joy - - - - - ful in the Lord, _____ be joy - - - ful all ___ ye lands, _____ all _____

5

89
Lord, be joy-ful, be joy-ful, be joy-ful all ye
Lord, be joy-ful, be joy-ful, be joy-ful all ye
Lord, be joy-ful, be joy-ful, be joy-ful all ye
89
92
lands, be joy - - - - - ful in the Lord,
lands, be joy - - - - - ful in the Lord,
lands, be joy - - - - - ful in the Lord,
92
95
be joy-ful in the Lord, all ye lands!
be joy - ful in the Lord, all ye lands!
be joy-ful in the Lord, all ye lands!
95

7

3. Serve the Lord with Gladness

110
come be - - - fore his
114
pre - - - - - sence with a song,
118
and come be - - - -
122
fore his pre - - - - - sence
126
with a song,
128
serve the Lord with glad - - -

130
serve the Lord with
serve the Lord with glad - - - ness, and
- - - - - - - - - - - ness,
130
133
glad - - - - ness, with glad - - - - ness, and
come be - - - fore his pre - - -
and come be - - -
133
137
come be - - - fore his
- - - sence, serve the Lord, with glad - ness,
fore his pre - sence with a
137

141
143
pre - - - - sence with a song,
song, serve the Lord with glad - - - -
145
serve the Lord with glad - - - - - - - ness,
and come be - - - -
- - - ness, and
148
serve the Lord with glad - - - - - ness, and
fore his pre - - - - - -
come be - - - fore his

come be - fore his pre - sence with a song.

- - - - - sence with a song.

pre - - - - - sence with a song.

4. Be Ye Sure that the Lord is God

Be ye sure that the Lord he is God,

Be ye sure that the Lord he is God, _____

165
Be ye sure that the Lord he is God,
Be ye sure that the Lord he is God,
165
1
167
it is he that has made
it is he
167
3
3
169
us, it is he that has made us, that has made us, it is he that has
us, it is he that has made us, that he made us, it is
169

made _____ us, and not we our-selves, and not we our selves, _____

he that has made _____ us, and not we our - selves, and not we our-

_____ not we _____ our - selves;

selves, _____ not we our - selves;

we are his

we are his peo - ple

181
peo-ple and the sheep of his pas - ture, we are his
and the sheep of his pas - - - - ture,
181
184
peo - - - ple and the sheep and the sheep, and the sheep of his
we are his peo - ple and the - sheep of his pas - - - - -
184
187
pas - - - - - - - - - ture.
- - - - - - - - - - - ture.
187
f
190

5. O Go Your Way Into His Gates

O go your way in-to his gates, O

O go your way in - to his gates with

O go your way in - to his

go your way in - to his gates with thanks - giv - ing,

thank - giv - ing, with thanks - giv - ing,

gates with thanks-giv-ing, with thanks - giv - ing,

O go your way in to his gates with

O go your way in to his gates with

O go your way in to his gates

thanks - - - - - - - giv - ing, with -

thanks - - - - - - giv - ing, with

with thanks - - -

229
thanks - giv - ing, with thanks - giv - ing,
thanks - - - - - - - - - - - -
giv - ing, O
229
5
235
with thanks - - - - - giv
- - - - - giv - ing, with thanks - - -
go your way in - to his gates with thanks -
235
2
2
2
241
243
ing, and in - to his courts with praise,
giv - ing, and in - to his courts with
giv - ing,
241
243

246
praise,
and in - to his courts with praise,
246
252
and in - to his courts with praise,
and in - to his courts with
and in - to his courts with
252
258
and in - to his courts with praise,
praise,
and in - to his courts with praise,
praise,
258

264
with praise, and in - to his courts with praise,
with praise, and in - to his courts, and in -
with praise,
264
mp
270
271
O go your way in - to his gates,
to his courts with praise,
O go your way in - to his gates with
270
271
f
276
and in - to his courts with praise,
with praise,
thanks - giv - ing, and in - to his courts with praise,
276

282
288
with praise:
with praise: be thankful
with praise: be
289
be thankful unto him, and speak good of his name, be
unto him, and speak good of his name,
thankful unto him, and speak good of his name, be thankful
296
thankful unto him, and speak good of his name, of his
be thankful unto him, and speak good of his
unto him, and speak good of his

303
name, be thank - ful un - - - to him, and
name, be thank - ful un - - - to him, and speak good
name,
303
3
3
4
3
309
speak good of his name, and speak good
of his name, be thank - ful un - - - to him, and
be thank - ful un - - - to him, and speak good
309
4
315
318
of his name, and
speak good of his name, be thank - ful un - to him, and
of his name, be thank - ful
315
3
318
3

321
speak good of his name, of his name, be thank - ful
speak good of his name, of his name, be
un - to him, and speak good of his name,
321
3
3
327
un - to him, and speak good of his name, of
thank - ful un - to him, and speak good of his name,
be thank - ful un - to him, and speak good of -
327
333
334
his name and speak good of his name,
of his name, and speak good of his name
- - his name, and speak good of his
333
334
5
2

338
and speak good of his name
and speak good of his name
name, of his name, be
338
4
344
be thank - ful un - to him, be thank - ful un - to
be thank - ful - un - to him
thank - ful un - to him, un - to him and speak good
344
350
him and speak good of his name, of his name.
and speak good of his name, of his name.
of his name, of his name.
350

6. For the Lord is Gracious

368
gra - cious, is gra - cious, is gra - cious, is gra - cious, his
is gra - cious, is gra - cious, is gra - cious, is gra - cious,
368
370
mer - - - - cy is e - ver - last - ing, is
his mer - cy is e - ver - last - - - - ing,
370
4
372
e - - ver - last - - - - - - ing,
his mer - cy is e - ver - last - - - ing,
Basso Solo
For the
372
5
2
3

the Lord is gra-cious, is gra-cious, is gra-cious,

the Lord is gra-cious, is gra-cious, is gra-cious,

Lord is gra-cious, is gra-cious, is gra-cious, his

his mer-cy e-ver-last-ing, his mer-cy is e-ver-

his mer-cy is e-ver-last-ing, his mer-cy, is e-ver-

mercy is e-ver-last-ing, his mer-cy, is e-ver-last-ing,

last-ing, his mer-cy is e-ver-last-ing,

last-ing, his mer-cy is e-ver-last ing,

his mer-cy, his mer-cy, is e-ver-last - - -

380
for the Lord is gra - cious,
for the Lord is gra - cious, his
380
382
his mer - cy is e - ver -
mer - cy is e - ver - last
382
384
last - ing,
ing,
ing,
and his
384

387
and his truth en - dures from ge-ne - ra - tion to ge - ne -
and his truth en -
truth en - dures from ge-ne - ra - - - - - tion to ge - ne -
387
p
390
ra - tion, from ge - ne - ra - - tion to ge - ne -
dures from ge - ne - ra - - - tion to ge - ne - ra - - -
ra - - - tion, and his truth en - dures from ge - ne - ra-tion to ge - ne -
390
393
ra - - - - - - tion, from ge - ne - ra -
- - - - - - tion, from
ra - - - tion, and his truth en - dures from ge - ne - ra -
393

396
- tion to ge - - - - ne - ra - tion, from ge - ne -
ge - ne - ra - - - tion to ge - ne - ra - tion, from ge - ne -
- tion to ge - ne - ra - - - - - tion, from ge - ne -
396
399
ra - tion to ge - - ne - ra - tion.
ra - tion to ge - - ne - ra - tion.
ra - tion to ge - - - ne-ra - tion.
399
403

7. Glory to the Father

418
Glo - - - - - - - - - - - ry,
Glo - - - - - - - - - - - ry,
Glo - - - - - - - - - - - ry,
418
4 1 4 3 5 4
422
glo - -
glo - -
glo - -
422
f
427
- - - - - - - - ry,
- - - - - - - - ry,
- - - - - - - - ry,
427
4 2 1 1

431
434
glo - - -
glo - - -
glo - - -
431
434
pp
f
435
- - - - ry
be
- - - - ry
be
- - - - ry
be
435
439
to the Fa - ther, glo - - -
to the Fa - ther, glo - - -
to the Fa - ther, glo - - -
439

443
ry, glo - ry be to the Son,
ry, glo - ry be to Son,
ry, glo - ry be to Son,
447
and to the ho - ly
and to the ho - - -
and to the ho - ly
451
Ghost
Ghost
Ghost
p

34

8. As It Was In the Begining

As it was in the be-gin-ing, is now, and e-ver shall be world with-out end, A -

A - - - - - - - - - men, A -

A - - - - - - - - - men, A -

men, A - - - - - - - - men, A -

men, as it was in the be - gin-ing, is now, and e-ver shall be world with-out end,

men,

men,

469
470
A - men, A - - - - - - - - - - men,
A - - - - - - - - - - -
A - - - - - - - -
469
470
473
as it was in the be - gin - ing, is now, and e-ver shall be world with -
men, A -
men,
473
477
out end, A - men, A - - - - - - -
- - - - men, as it was in the be - gin - ing, is now, and e-ver shall
477

481
484
men, A - - men, A-
be world with-out end, A - - - - - men, A-
A - - - - - - - men, as it was in
481
484
485
- men, A -
men, A -
the be - gin - ing, is now, and e-ver shall be world with-out end, as it
485
489
men,
men, A -
was in the be - gin - ing, is now, and e-ver shall be world with - out end,
489

493
A - men, A - - - - - - - - - - - men, A -
- - men, A - - - - - - - - - men, world with-
A - men, A - - - - - - - - - - - - - - -
493
5
497
498
- - - - - - men, A - - - - - - - - -
out end, A - men A - men, A - - - - - - - - -
- - - men, as it was in the be - gin - ing, is now, and e - ver shall
497
498
3
501
- men, A - men, A - - - - - - - - -
- - - - - - men, A - - - - - - - -
be world with - out end, A - men, A - -
501
4

38

517
518
- - men, A - - - - - men,
- - men, A - - - - - men,
be, A - - - - - men,
517
518
521
A - - - - - men,
A - - - - - men,
A - - - - - men,
521
525
526
as it was in the be - gin - ing, is now, and e - ver, is now, and
as it was in the be - gin - ing, is now, and e - ver, is now, and
as it was in the be - gin - ing, is now, and e - ver, is now, end
525
526

529
e - ver, and e - ver shall be, and e - ver, e - ver shall be world with-out
e - ver, and e - ver shall be, and e - ver, e - ver shall be world with-out
e - ver, and e - ver shall be, and e - ver, e - ver shall be world with-out
529
534
540 Adagio
end, world with-out end, with-out end,
end, world with-out end, with-out end, A -
end, world with-out end, with-out end, A -
534
540 Adagio
541
A - - - - men, A - - - - men, A - men.
- - - - men, A - - - men, A - men.
- - - men, A - - - - - - men, A - men.
541